WE·THE PEOPLE

HOUGHTON MIFFLIN

Let's Read

Biography

HOUGHTON MIFFLIN • Boston
Atlanta • Dallas • Geneva, Illinois • Palo Alto • Princeton

WE·THE PEOPLE

Let's Read
Biography

Photography Credits—

Cover and Title Page: *Left to Right from Top to Bottom*
Bethune-Cookman College, Office of Public Relations; The Granger Collection, New York; The Granger Collection, New York; (illustration) Chuck Passarelli/American Artists; (detail) National Portrait Gallery, Smithsonian Institution/Art Resource, NY; ©Flip Schulke/Black Star; ©SuperStock; Courtesy of Gary Soto; ©1996 Cradoc Bagshaw; ©Richard Howard/Black Star; (detail) Archives Division–Texas State Library; NASA.

AP/Wide World Photos, vi(t); (detail) Archives Division–Texas State Library, iii(c), vii(cr); ©1996 Cradoc Bagshaw, iii(l), vii(tr); Bethune-Cookman College, Office of Public Relations, iii(br), v(t)(tl); The Bettmann Archive, vi(b); ©Bob Fitch/Black Star, vi(r); The Granger Collection, New York, ii(cr), iii(tr), v(cr)(bl)(b), vii(b); ©Richard Howard/Black Star, ii(tl), vii(cl); NASA, ii(br), vii(bl); (detail) National Portrait Gallery, Smithsonian Institution/Art Resource, NY, ii(bl), vi(cl); Dennis O'Clair/Tony Stone Images, x–xi; ©Barbara Peacock 1992/FPG International, x; Photoreporters, Inc., ix; Donovan Reese/Tony Stone Images, xii–xiii; ©Steve Satushek/The Image Bank, xii–xiii; ©Flip Schulke/Black Star, ii(bc), vi(cr); Courtesy of Gary Soto, iii(tl), vi(br); Don Spiro/Tony Stone Images, xi; ©SuperStock, ii(cl), vi(bl); UPI/Bettmann Newsphotos, vii(t); Terry Vine/Tony Stone Images, viii.

Mary McLeod Bethune
Bethune Museum & Archives, 3(tl); Bethune-Cookman College, Office of Public Relations, 1, 2(b), 3(b), 4(t), 5, 6(b), 9(cr)(r), 12(t); The Bettmann Archive, 12(b); Photo by Wilbert Blanche/Culver Pictures, 7(b); Culver Pictures, 3(tr); Howard University, 4(b); The National Archives, 2(t); National Portrait Gallery, Smithsonian Institution/Art Resource, NY, 12(c); PhotoDisc Images ©1995 PhotoDisc, Inc., 10(tr)(cl)(cr), 11(tr); Photographs and Prints Division, Schomburg Center, New York Public Library, 7(t); UPI/Bettmann, 8; UPI/Bettmann Newsphotos, 6(t).

Helen Keller
The American Foundation for the Blind, 14(b), 17, 18, 20(t), 22(l), 24 top to bottom(1); AP/Wide World Photos, 15; The Bettmann Archive, 19(t)(bl); The Granger Collection, New York, 13; Perkins School for the Blind, 14(t), 16, 20(b), 21, 24 top to bottom(2); PhotoDisc Images ©1995 PhotoDisc, Inc., 19(br); UPI/Bettmann, 22(r), 24 top to bottom(3)(4)(5)(6); UPI/Bettmann Newsphotos, 19(br); UPI/Bettmann/The American Foundation for the Blind, 24 top to bottom(7).

Christopher Columbus
The Bettmann Archive, 35(tl)(cl)(br); The Granger Collection, New York, 25, 28, 29, 30–31, 32, 35(tc)(tr)(c)(cr)(bl); The Mariners' Museum, 26; National Maritime Museum London, 27(c), 30(t); PhotoDisc Images ©1995 PhotoDisc, Inc., 27(b), 30(bl), 34, 35(b); Scala/Art Resource, NY, 35(bc); ©Stock Montage, 25(bkg), 36.

The acknowledgments for this product, which continue on page 145, are considered to be an extension of this copyright page.

Contents

American Voices

We are proud of ourselves,
our families, our communities,
our country!

We care about our neighbors
and our neighborhood.
We play by the rules.
We are fair.

$\mathcal{W}$e try as hard as
we can to be
good readers and writers,
good workers, and
good citizens.

We love our flag
wherever it flies!

"Let Freedom Ring"

We are the

Spirit of America!

Mary
McLeod
Bethune

As a child, Mary McLeod picked cotton on her father's farm.

▲ Cotton pickers in the south

▲ Mary was born in this house.

2

Mary wanted to learn to read. She was a good student.

MAYESVILLE INDUSTRIAL INSTITUTE

▲ Emma J. Wilson opened a school. Mary learned to read there.

▲ Mary spent years studying.

▶ She was in her twenties when this photo was taken.

Mary wanted to teach African American children to read and write.

▲ Mary with her teachers and students

▶ Mary asked many people to help pay for a new school.

She opened a school in Daytona Beach, Florida, for African American children.

▲ Mary visited a school for African American children.

Mary spoke about a world garden, where flowers of all colors grew.

Mary believed that people were like wonderful, colorful flowers in the world. One of Mary's favorite flowers was a black tulip. It showed that the world garden had colors for everyone.

Mary started a small hospital. Then she built an even bigger one.

Mary is shown here discussing the training of African American Army women.

Monument to Mary McLeod Bethune in Washington, D.C.

Mary became famous and spoke all around the country.

Mary helped young people become the best they could be.

Mary cared about all Americans.

▲ **Mary looks on as President Truman signs a bill proclaiming National Freedom Day.**

◄ **Mary and Eleanor Roosevelt became good friends.**

Let's Explore!

Put your finger on the town where Mary was born. Tell which direction you would travel to get to the place where she started her own school.

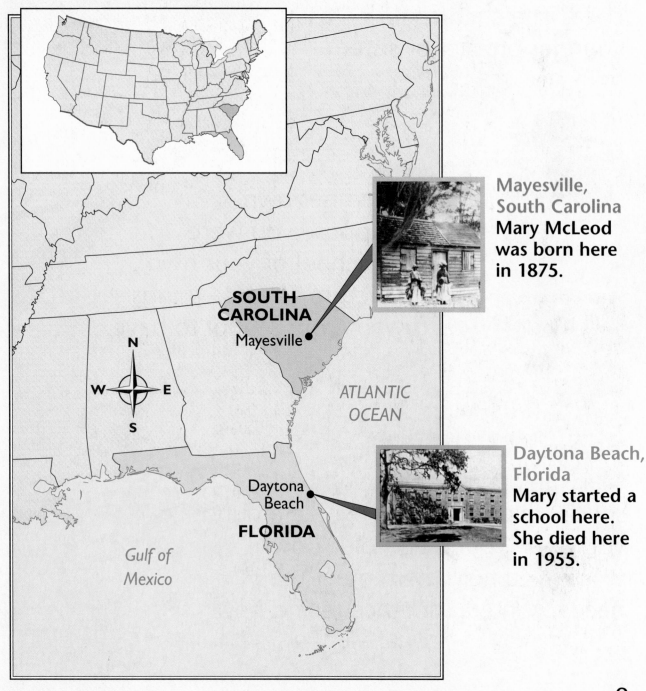

Mayesville, South Carolina
Mary McLeod was born here in 1875.

SOUTH CAROLINA
Mayesville

ATLANTIC OCEAN

N
W   E
S

Daytona Beach
FLORIDA

Gulf of Mexico

Daytona Beach, Florida
Mary started a school here. She died here in 1955.

What Do You Think?

Teaching Others

Write about something you can do well. Tell how you could teach it to another child. The child could be a younger brother or sister.

My Own School

Mary started her own school. Suppose you were starting a school of your own. Draw a picture of some things you'd want your school to have.

SPECIAL NEEDS

Mary helped children who had special needs. Look at people around you, both young and old. How would you help them meet their needs? Write a sentence telling how.

THE LEARNING PATH

Children graduated from Mary's schools. How many times do you think you will graduate from a school?

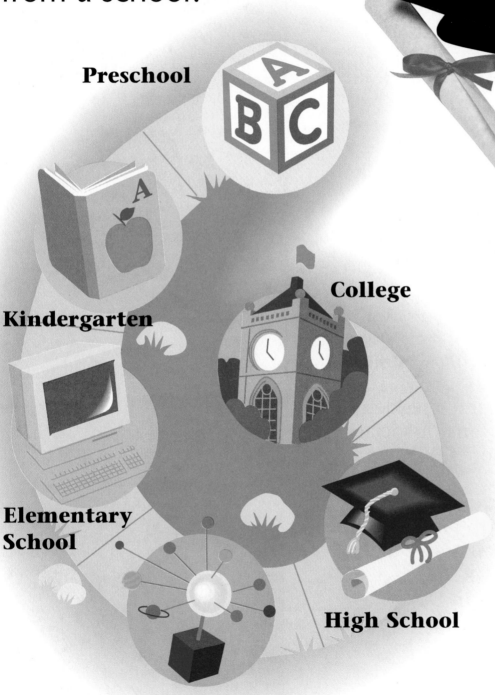

Preschool

Kindergarten

College

Elementary School

High School

Middle School

Key Events

1875 Mary McLeod was born in Mayesville, South Carolina.

1884 She entered Miss Emma Wilson's school and learned to read.

1894 She entered Moody Bible Institute in Chicago, Illinois.

1898 She married Albertus Bethune.

1903 She moved to Daytona Beach, Florida, and taught school.

1904 She opened a school for African American girls.

1924 She became president of the National Association for Colored Women.

1935 She became a special adviser to President Roosevelt.

1955 She died in Daytona Beach, Florida.

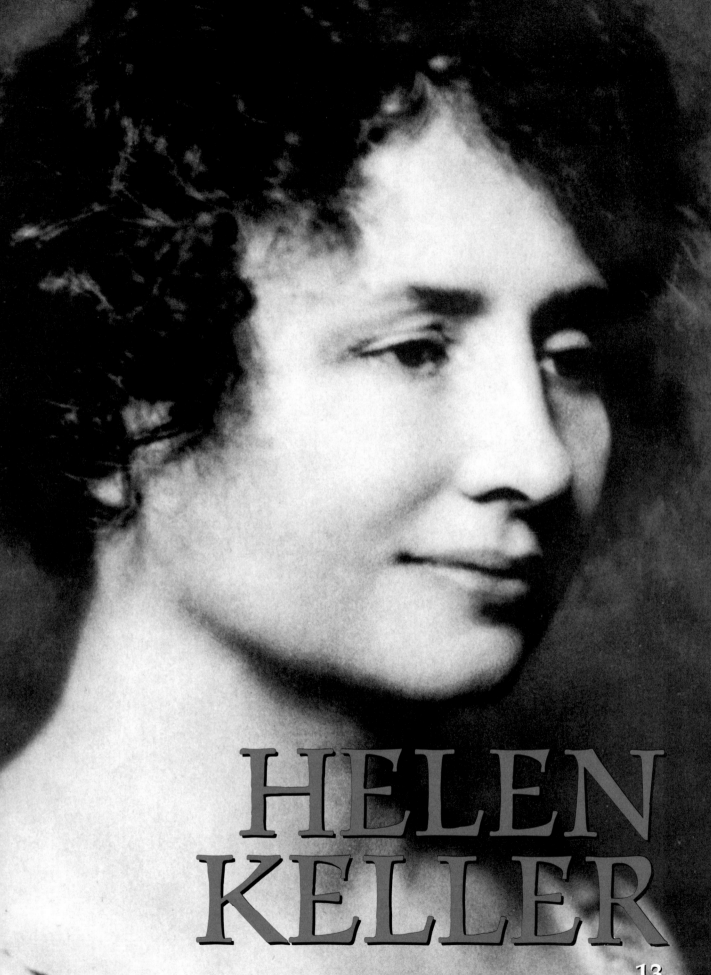

HELEN
KELLER

13

Helen Keller could not see, hear, or speak.

▲ Young Helen uses her fingers to read.

▶ Helen's father wanted to find a teacher for her.

Annie Sullivan was Helen Keller's teacher.

▲ Helen with Annie Sullivan

Annie taught Helen many words.

▲ Helen touched Annie's lips to "hear" her words.

What is Braille?
A young man named Louis Braille could not see. He figured out a way for people who could not see to "read." Raised dots stand for different letters and sounds. People feel the dots and read with their fingers. Braille is like a code. Here are the letters of Helen Keller's name in the Braille alphabet.

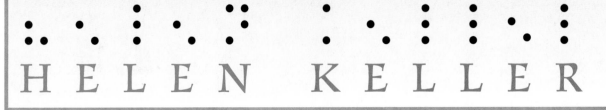

Helen learned that words have meanings.

▲ Helen reading a Braille book

17

Helen learned to speak and type her words.
She went to college.

▲ Helen went to Radcliffe College. She worked very hard to learn the way
everyone else did. She is shown here studying geometry.

Helen and Annie gave speeches and wrote books together.

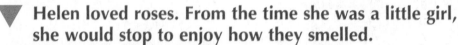
Helen loved roses. From the time she was a little girl, she would stop to enjoy how they smelled.

Both Helen and Annie wanted to help people have a better life.

Like everyone else, Helen needed money to buy food, clothes, and a place to live. She had many jobs. She wrote books, performed on stage, and gave speeches.

Let's Explore!

Helen went to Perkins School. Look at the map. It shows some of the school's buildings. How could you get from the children's house to the head teacher's house?

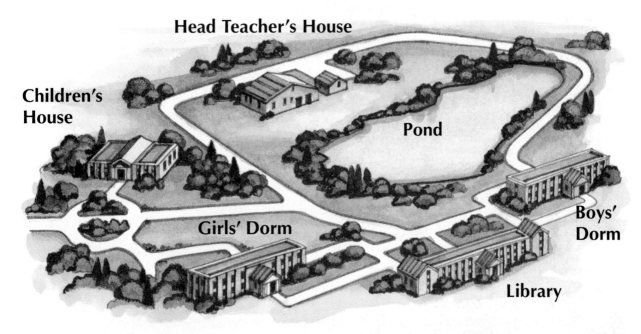

Head Teacher's House

Children's House

Pond

Girls' Dorm

Boys' Dorm

Library

Perkins School then and now

What Do You Think?

I Am a Star!
List some things that you do well. Put a star next to what you do best. Tell what you do well. Now, draw a picture of yourself being a star!

I Care, Too!
Helen helped many children who could not see or hear. You can help others, too. You could tell stories, teach games, or just be a friend to someone who needs one. Tell how you could help.

Pet Pals

Helen Keller loved dogs. From the time she was a little girl until she was very old, she almost always had a dog. Think of ways that pets are our pals. Draw a picture of your favorite pet.

The Braille Alphabet

a	b	c	d	e
f	g	h	i	j
k	l	m	n	o
p	q	r	s	t
u	v	x	y	z
and	for	of	the	with
ch	gh	sh	th	wh
ed	er	ou	ow	w

Helen as a young girl

Annie Sullivan

Helen and Annie

Helen with Alexander Graham Bell

Helen and Annie

Helen in 1915

Helen in 1960

Key Events

Helen Keller was born on June 27, 1880.

Annie Sullivan was born in 1866.

Annie Sullivan began teaching Helen Keller when Helen was almost seven.

Helen Keller graduated from Radcliffe College in 1904.

Annie Sullivan married John Macy.

Annie and Helen toured the world giving speeches.

Helen Keller wrote many books.

Annie Sullivan died in 1936.

Helen Keller died in 1968.

Christopher Columbus

Christopher Columbus was a sea captain.

He wanted to find a route to Asia by sailing west.

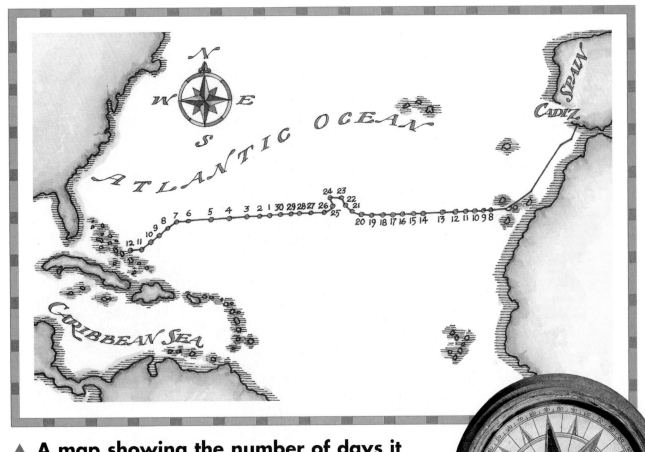

▲ A map showing the number of days it took for Columbus's first trip

▶ A compass like the one Columbus might have used

A compass was used to find out in what direction the ship was going.

The king and queen of Spain gave Columbus three ships.

▶ Columbus and his crew sailed three ships called the *Niña,* the *Pinta,* and the *Santa María.*

In 1492 Christopher Columbus sailed
from Spain.

▲ **Columbus and his crew worked as a team to sail the ships.**

The trip was hard. It lasted many weeks.

A sandglass was used to measure time.

▶ **A sandglass from long ago**

▲ **A modern sandglass**

"Land Ho!" a sailor shouted on October 12, 1492. The crew saw land. It was an island off the coast of North America.

Later Columbus sailed across the ocean three more times. He thought the land he explored was near Asia.

Let's Explore!

The map shows Columbus's first trip. So does the picture of the globe. When would you use a map? When would you use a globe?

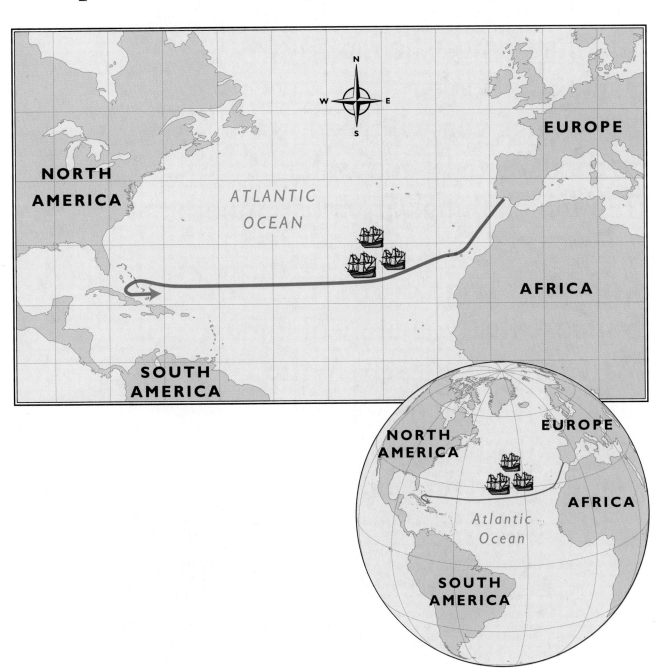

What Do You Think?

A Long Trip

You are a sailor.
You are going on a long trip.
What will you take with you?
List fun things such as toys,
games, or books.
List things you will need, such
as food, clothes, and water.
Tell which things are most important.

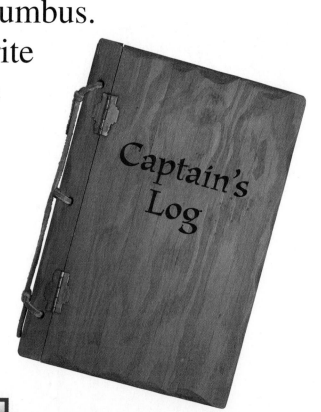

Captain's Log

Suppose that you are Columbus.
Write about your day. Write
about what you do on the
ship. Tell what you think
you will find on land.

A Man of Many Faces

No one is sure what Columbus looked like.
See how different he looks in each painting!

If you were an artist, how
would you draw
Christopher Columbus?

Key Events

1451 Christopher Columbus was born.

1465 Columbus went to sea and learned how to sail.

1486 Columbus told King Ferdinand and Queen Isabella about his sailing plans.

1492 Finally, King Ferdinand and Queen Isabella agreed to Columbus's plan. On the first trip, he landed on an island off the coast of North America.

1493 He sailed on a second trip. He landed on Hispaniola.

1498 Columbus sailed on a third trip. He landed on South America.

1502 Columbus sailed on a fourth trip. He landed on Central America.

1506 Columbus died in Spain.

SQUANTO

Squanto was a Native American.

He and his people farmed the land and fished the waters.

Basket

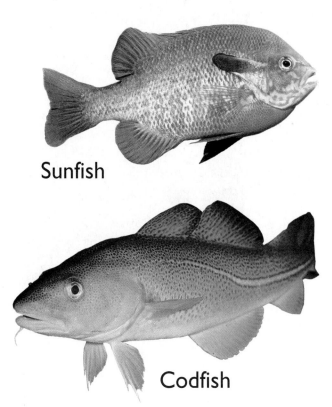
Sunfish

Codfish

One day a ship came carrying settlers.

The *Mayflower*

They were the Pilgrims.

The Pilgrims landed in Plymouth in 1620.

The first winter was hard for the Pilgrims.

Soon Pilgrims began to build warm houses.

Squanto taught these settlers what he knew about living on the land.

Pilgrims learned how Native Americans stored their corn.

Squanto put fish under the seeds to help the corn grow.

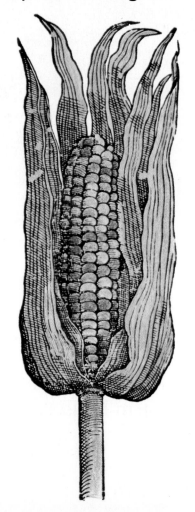

He showed them new ways of planting.

Today, at a place called Plimoth Plantation, people act out the lives of the first New England colonists and the Native Americans. Visitors go to the living history museum to learn about early times in America.

The Pilgrims were thankful for Squanto's help. The Pilgrims, Squanto, and other Native Americans enjoyed a feast together in the fall of 1621.

The First Thanksgiving

What might be served at a New England Thanksgiving feast today?

Let's Explore!

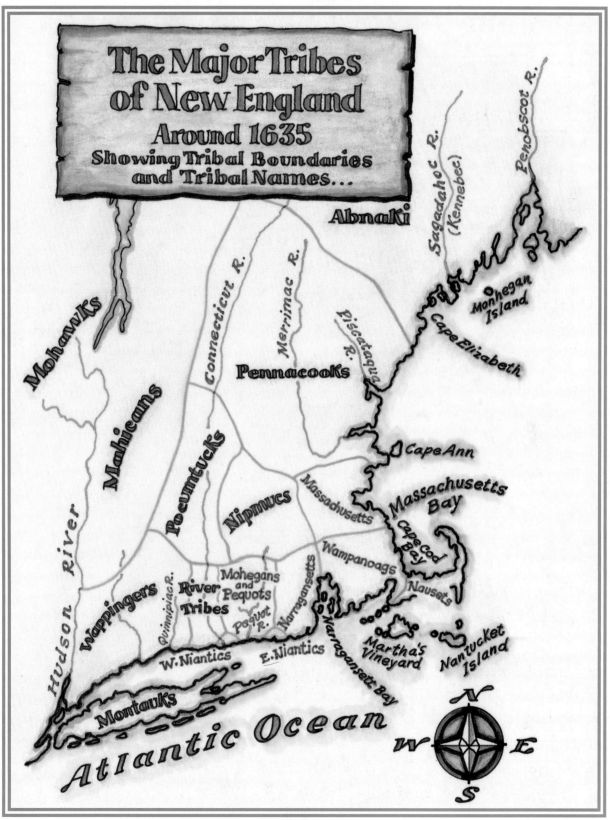

The Major Tribes of New England Around 1635
Showing Tribal Boundaries and Tribal Names...

Abnaki

Sagadahoc R. (Kennebec)

Penobscot R.

Monhegan Island

Cape Elizabeth

Mohawks

Connecticut R.

Merrimac R.

Piscataqua R.

Pennacooks

Mahicans

Cape Ann

Pocumtucks

Massachusetts

Massachusetts Bay

Nipmucs

Wampanoags

Cape Cod Bay

Nausets

Hudson river

Wappingers

Quinipiac R.

River Tribes

Mohegans and Pequots

Pequot R.

Narragansetts

W. Niantics

E. Niantics

Narragansett Bay

Martha's Vineyard

Nantucket Island

Montauks

Atlantic Ocean

N
W   E
S

What Do You Think?

A FRIEND

Squanto was a friend to the Pilgrims. He taught them many things. Write about or draw a picture of Squanto helping the Pilgrims. Tell how he helped them.

PLAN A THANKSGIVING FEAST

The Pilgrims and Native Americans had many kinds of foods at their feast. Make a list of foods you would have at Thanksgiving.

My Thanksgiving List

Look Back in Time

The early Americans worked hard. How do you think they used objects like these shown here to help them?

English hoe

Native American storage bag

Native American harvest basket

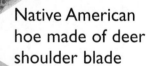

Native American hoe made of deer shoulder blade

Jawbone of deer used to remove green corn from ear

English carrying basket

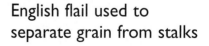

Husking peg used to separate husks from ears of corn

English flail used to separate grain from stalks

Key Events

Squanto was a Native American of the Pawtuxet tribe.

Squanto was captured by a sea captain and taken to England. There he learned English. He was freed and came back to America.

The Pilgrims went through a hard winter. Squanto decided to help them.

Squanto taught the Pilgrims many things. One important thing was how to plant corn.

To celebrate their harvest, the Pilgrims invited Native American neighbors to a feast. It was a feast of thanksgiving.

Squanto died about a year later.

THOMAS EDISON

Thomas Edison was an inventor.

Thomas Edison's laboratory

One of his inventions was the electric light bulb.

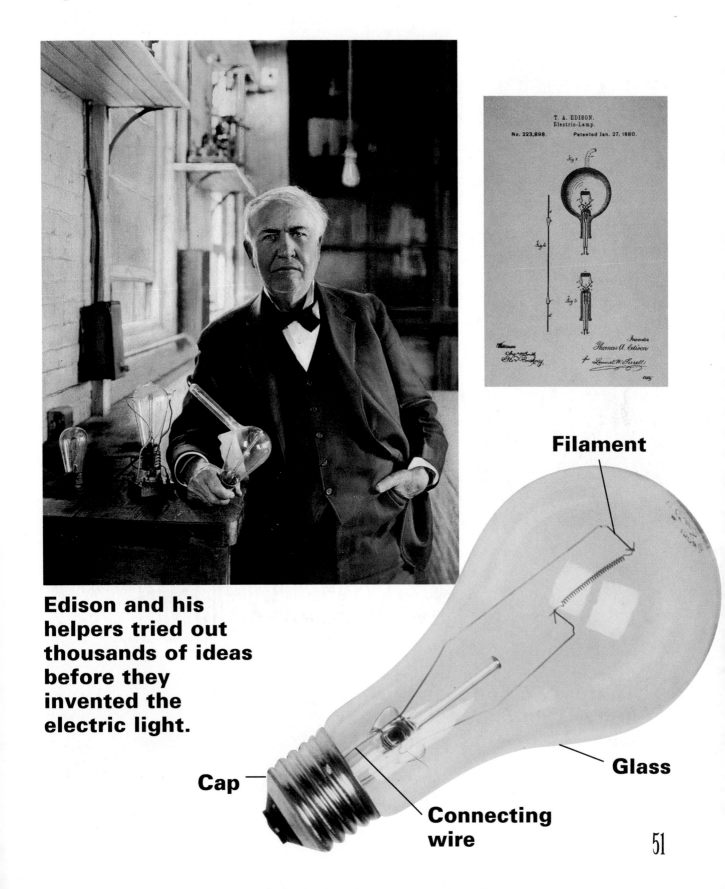

T. A. EDISON.
Electric-Lamp.
No. 223,898.   Patented Jan. 27, 1880.

Edison and his helpers tried out thousands of ideas before they invented the electric light.

Filament

Glass

Cap

Connecting wire

Thomas Edison always liked to ask questions.

At age thirteen, Thomas sold newspapers and candy on a train. He set up a lab in a boxcar and did experiments in his free time.

Thomas Edison was born in 1847. This photo was taken when he was 33 years old.

He wanted to know how things worked.

Thomas Edison experimented with machines that recorded sounds. He invented the phonograph.

Thomas Edison invented new machines and made other machines work better.

Edison with an early motion picture camera

Thomas Edison in his New York laboratory

Edison hired others to help him turn his ideas into inventions.

He used teamwork to build machines and invent many things. Over the years he had several laboratories.

Thomas Edison listening to a phonograph

Edison talking into one of his inventions

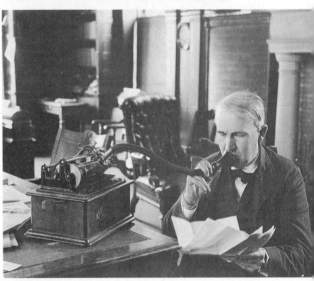

Thomas Edison's great ideas changed the lives of all Americans.

Edison and his team invented the movie projector.

Let's Explore!

Thomas Edison was born in Milan, Ohio. When he was seven years old, he moved to Port Huron, Michigan. What direction is Port Huron from Milan? What river is close to Port Huron?

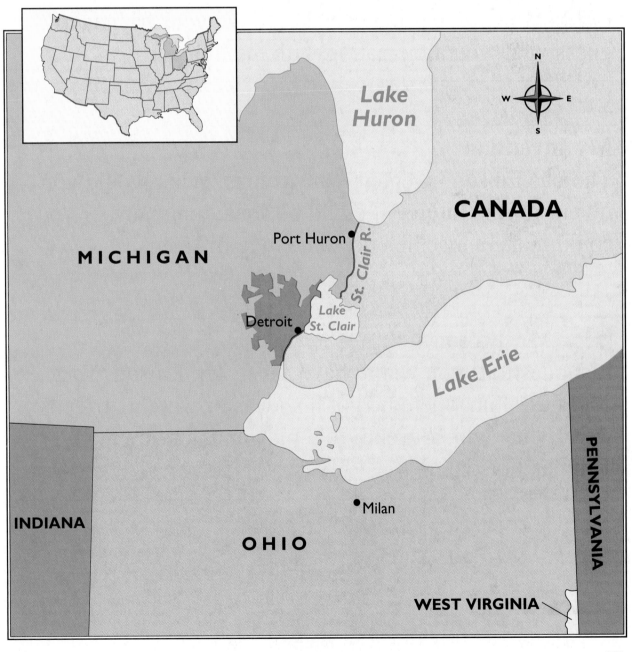

What Do You Think?

Shadow Play

Using an electric light, create a shadow play. Shine the light on a white wall or screen. In front of the light, make shadow puppets using your fingers. See how many different puppets you can make. Invite your friends to guess what you are creating with the light.

My Invention

Thomas Edison invented many things. What would you invent for the future? It could be something new, or you could make a machine do something different.

Dear Mr. Edison

List questions you would have asked Mr. Edison. You could ask him where he got his ideas or who his friends were. Then with a friend, role-play an interview with Thomas Edison.

INVENTIONS AND FRIENDS!

Thomas Edison was friends with Henry Ford, another great inventor of the time. Ford invented the automobile.

Edison and Ford look at Edison's light bulbs.

Ford (far left) and Edison (second from left) were two of President Harding's guests in 1922.

Ford helps Edison celebrate his 80th birthday.

Four friends visit an antique mill wheel. From left, Thomas Edison, John Burroughs, Henry Ford, and Henry Firestone

59

More about Thomas Edison

Thomas Edison was born in 1847.

Thomas was hearing impaired. This lack of hearing allowed him to focus on his inventing.

Thomas was forgetful about some things. He sometimes forgot what day it was.

Thomas nicknamed a daughter Dot and a son Dash after the Morse code.

Thomas received the Congressional Medal of Honor in 1928.

Thomas died in 1931. On the evening of Edison's funeral, lights were dimmed across the United States.

Martin Luther King, Jr.

Martin Luther King, Jr. had a dream.

This picture shows Martin and his family in 1939. Martin is the child at the right.

Martin Luther King, Jr. was born in this house on January 15, 1929.

He dreamed of freedom.

On August 28, 1963, Martin Luther King, Jr. led the March on Washington for Jobs and Freedom.

Martin Luther King, Jr. spoke about freedom.

He marched for freedom.

👆 Martin Luther King, Jr. led civil rights workers to Montgomery, Alabama.

Martin Luther King, Jr. wanted freedom for everyone.

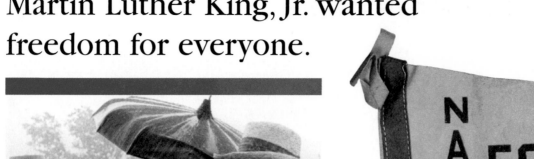

People marched for freedom in all kinds of weather.

He worked for freedom.

☞ Dr. King spoke to thousands of people in Washington, D.C., on August 28, 1963.

☝ Between 3000–5000 people marched with Dr. King from Selma to Montgomery, Alabama, in March 1965. The march took five days.

Martin Luther King, Jr. dreamed of freedom for all people. His dream is our dream.

Let's Explore!

African Americans and whites marched together from Selma to Montgomery, Alabama. Use your finger to trace the way they walked.

Martin Luther King, Jr. points to Selma, Alabama, where the march began.

What Do You Think?

My Dream

What would you like to be when you grow up? Write about it. Tell why it is your dream job.

A Leader Is

Dr. Martin Luther King, Jr. was a leader. He did many things. Write down three things you think a leader should do. Then name someone you think is a leader.

From the Family Album

Martin at a birthday party

Martin's wife, Coretta, and their four children

Martin and his family

The King family eating dinner

Key Events

1929 Martin Luther King, Jr. was born in Atlanta, Georgia, on January 15.

1948 He graduated from Morehouse College.

1953 He married Coretta Scott.

1963 He delivered the "I Have a Dream" speech at the march on Washington.

1965 He led the march from Selma to Montgomery.

1968 He was killed in Memphis, Tennessee, on April 4.

Martin Luther King, Jr. won the Nobel Prize for peace.

George Washington

George Washington was the first President of the United States. He was a great leader.

George Washington took the oath of office in New York City. He promised to defend the Constitution.

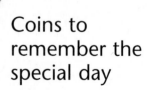

Coins to remember the special day

Before he became President, George did many things.

He was a land surveyor.

He was a colonel in the
Virginia Militia.

George
Washington
loved music.
This artist has
shown him
playing the
flute.

George Washington was the general and leader of the United States Army.

This famous painting shows General Washington and his soldiers crossing the Delaware River.

Leading his soldiers

This was a special merit badge George Washington gave to soldiers.

George Washington led many battles against Great Britain.

Often George Washington's troops went hungry and barefoot in the snow.

Helping a soldier

Each star on this flag from long ago stands for one of the original 13 colonies.

He helped the United States win its freedom from Great Britain.

At the Constitutional Convention in Philadelphia

George Washington was a great leader.
He is called the Father of His Country.

Let's Explore!

This map shows Mount Vernon, Virginia, where George Washington lived. Read the key. Find out what each number means.

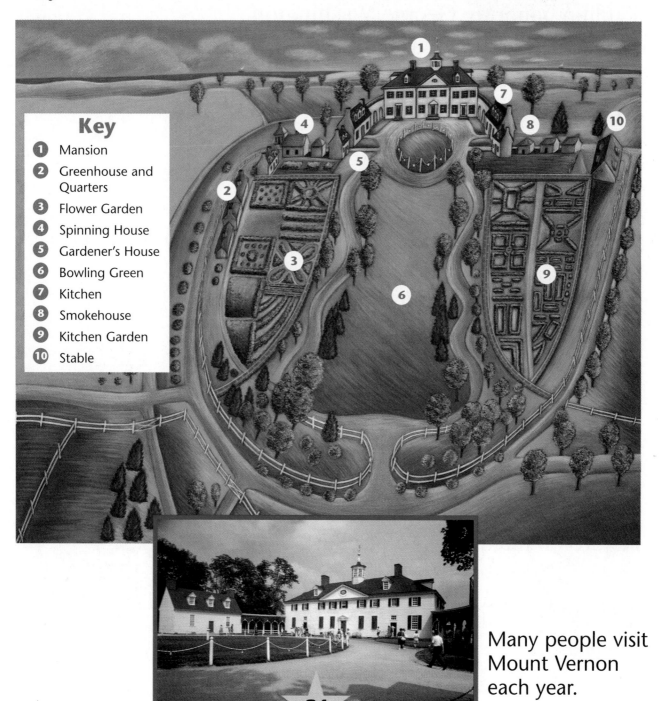

Key

1. Mansion
2. Greenhouse and Quarters
3. Flower Garden
4. Spinning House
5. Gardener's House
6. Bowling Green
7. Kitchen
8. Smokehouse
9. Kitchen Garden
10. Stable

Many people visit Mount Vernon each year.

81

What Do You Think?

George Washington Stamp

Washington's face appears on many things such as stamps and coins. Create a stamp honoring George Washington. You could show him as a grown-up or as a child. Tell about your stamp and how much it costs.

The Washington Monument

The monument is slightly over 555 feet high and took longer than 36 years to build. Use clay or paper to make your own model of the Washington monument. Tell about the monument and what shape it is.

George's Name

Many places and things are named for George Washington. See how many things you can list that have George's name or his picture on them. Share your list with the class. Then see how many words you can make out of the 16 letters in his name.

ring
go
wash
ton

W A S H I N G T O N

A Special Man

George Washington was liked and respected. He was the subject of many artists' works.

by George Hicks

by Currier and Ives

by Gilbert Stuart

by John Trumbull

83

More About George Washington

George Washington was born in Virginia in 1732. He died in 1799.

He was over six feet tall, which was tall for his time.

As a young man, he was a land surveyor.

He married Martha Custis. She was a widow with two children.

He had sets of false teeth made from wood, from ivory, and even from hippopotamus tusk.

It's been said that one of his favorite foods was ice cream.

He loved his home, Mount Vernon, Virginia.

GARY
SOTO

... voice.

... good day to start your

... Novios of a Bday party!

... piñata with newspaper and cardboard.

... s and crayons, plus shoe strings. In no

... tiny sacks of cat treats.

... ed Blanco's Bakery and ordered a cake. He stuffed the piñata

... le of cat treats.

... mouse-brown frosting.

... le of canaries on top." Chato added.

... paws and dialed his friend Tiburon, a D.J. who

... own chicken coop.

... d. "You awake?"

... e said sleepily.

... tomorrow I want you to spin so come to ... up.

... three

85

Gary Soto writes books and poems.

Gary was born in Fresno, California. Here he is on the front porch with his friends.

This is Gary.

Gary (far right) with his brother, Rick, and his sister, Debra, in their backyard

Gary read some poetry in high school. "This is great!" he thought.

Here Gary cools off with his brother and sister.

This is Gary's report card from third grade.

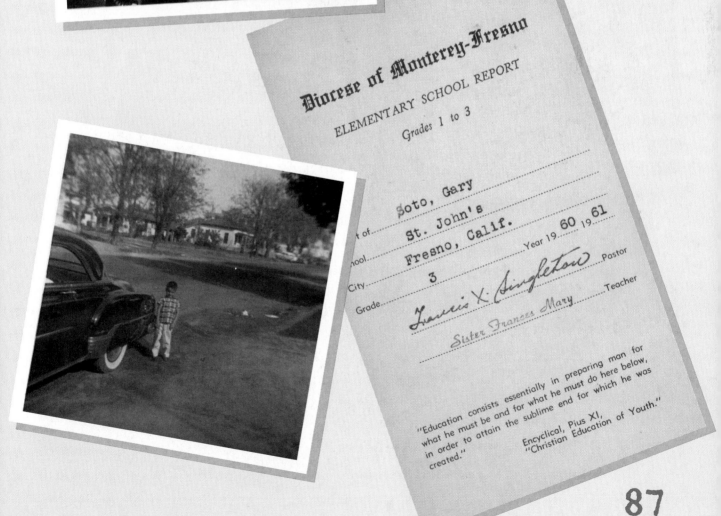

Diocese of Monterey-Fresno

ELEMENTARY SCHOOL REPORT

Grades 1 to 3

.... of .... Soto, Gary

.... ool .... St. John's

.... City .... Fresno, Calif.   Year 19..60.. 19..61..

.... Grade 3   *Francis X. Singleton* .... Pastor

.... *Sister Frances Mary* .... Teacher

"Education consists essentially in preparing man for what he must be and for what he must do here below, in order to attain the sublime end for which he was created."

Encyclical, Pius XI,
"Christian Education of Youth."

So Gary wrote his own poetry.

This is how Gary looked when he was twenty-one. He was writing poetry.

Gary likes to write in bed. Sometimes he uses a laptop computer.

Then Gary decided to write stories.

Gary's grandmother, Apolonia Soto, and Gary's grandfather, Francisco Soto, were both born in Mexico.

Gary wrote about his family and friends. This is Gary with his daughter, Mariko.

In his book, *Too Many Tamales,* Gary tells about a little girl. Gary has written many stories and poems for children and grown-ups.

Gary traveled to France. He was surprised to find a book he had written being sold in a French bookstore.

Gary is curious about many things. He enjoys going to museums. Here Gary is visiting an aviation museum.

Gary remembers things about growing up. Then he writes about them.

Gary visits many schools and meets a lot of children. Gary gets many letters, too. Here are two of them.

Dear Gary Soto,

Hello! My name is Belia. I am 12 years old. I really enjoy your books because they have a little bit of our culture, and I really like the words in Spanish. The book, _Pacific Crossing_ was great! I really enjoyed it because I'm Mexican and I take Kempo Karate like Lincoln. I also agree with Lincoln about Kempo being very tiring. I am a purple belt in kempo going on blue belt. I also like all of your poems like "Oranges", I like it because it has a lot of details and it is very sweet. You are one of my favorite authors. Thank you for taking time to read this letter.

P.S.
Your books are great!
I hope you write back soon.

Always,
Belia
Belia

Dear Mr. Soto,

Thank you for visiting our school on the date of October 3, 1995.

I really enjoyed your prese for us. I liked "La Bamba" the best. My nephew, whom is 4, heard "La Cocaracha", and when I told him what it meant, he laughed. So, if you ever visit little kids' schools, maybe you can sing that and tell them what it means.

I always thought that writers were smart people too unwise to realize a joke or listen to music. Seeing you, and how you acted, changed my mind. You listen to music, told jokes, and were smart. I like a person like that.

Sincerely,
Matthew

91

Gary has won awards for writing.
He says, "Read as much as you can!"

Gary used to teach karate.

Let's Explore!

Gary Soto was born in Fresno, California. Trace a path from Fresno to Berkeley. In which direction would you go?

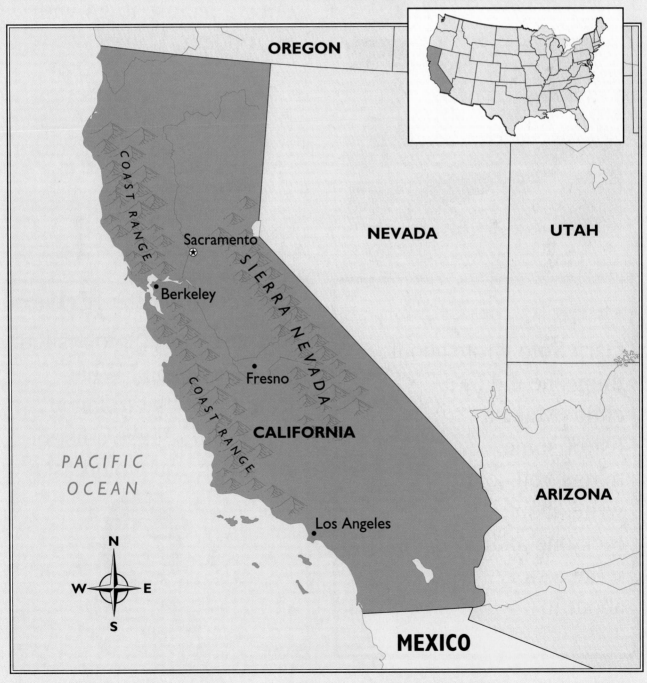

What Do You Think?

Reading Poetry

Share a poem you like. Write about what the poem means to you.

Be a Poet!

Gary Soto is a poet. Write a poem of your own. Then draw a picture to go with your poem.

My bike is new.
It's fast and fun.
I race up hills
To catch the sun.

IDEAS! IDEAS!

Gary Soto wrote about things he did as a child. Make a list of some things you could write about. Pick one and write a story about it.

Interview the Writer

Suppose Gary Soto visited your classroom. What would you like to know about him? Make a list of questions you would ask.

Welcome, Gary

Meet Corky!

Gary Soto likes animals. One of his most special friends is his cat, Corky. Here Gary and Corky spend the morning together.

Reading the newspaper

Corky's favorite breakfast is a hot bowl of oatmeal! Gary likes it, too.

And now it's time to play!

Key Events

1952 Gary Soto was born in Fresno, California.

1974 He graduated from California State University.

1975 He married Carolyn Oda.

1977 Gary's first book of poetry was published.

1985 Gary's first book of short stories was published.

Maria Martinez

Maria Martinez was a Tewa artist.
She made clay pots.

Maria and Julian, her
husband, at work

Water jar created by
Maria and Julian

She won many awards for her beautiful art.

Maria
examining a
finished pot

Maria Martinez worked in a small village in New Mexico.

She kept Pueblo traditions alive in the designs of her pots.

Maria lived in San Ildefonso Pueblo, New Mexico.

Comanche dance on feast day

Comanche dance

Buffalo dance

Maria Martinez taught her family and the people in her village how to make pots.

Maria takes clay from the earth.

She mixes the clay with gray sandstone.

Now many people in her family are carrying on that tradition. They make their living as artists in clay.

Adam and
Santana
Martinez,
potters

Plaza, San Ildefonso,
New Mexico

Maria Martinez introduced Pueblo pottery and traditions to the world. Maria Martinez has been called "Mother of the Pueblo."

Maria covers a pot with a thin gray paste.

Maria molds, or shapes, a pot.

Let's Explore!

Use the map key to find the capital city of New Mexico. In which direction is the capital city from San Ildefonso?

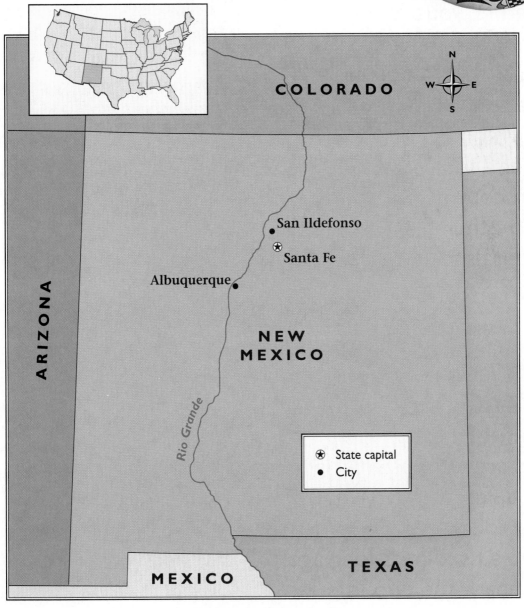

COLORADO

San Ildefonso

⊛ Santa Fe

Albuquerque

NEW MEXICO

ARIZONA

Rio Grande

⊛ State capital
• City

MEXICO

TEXAS

N
W E
S

What Do You Think?

Designs of Today
Draw a design for your class. Then decide whether you would want your design to be on a T-shirt, a poster, or a pot. Draw your design on paper and then copy it onto other materials.

Pottery Shapes
Look at the shapes of Maria's pottery. Pick a shape and use clay to make your own pot. You can add your design to it. Set your pot in a warm spot to dry. Give it to someone special.

Useful Pottery
Pots are very useful. List all the different ways we use pots today. In a group, list ways people used pots long ago. Compare the two lists.

LET'S MAKE A POT!

1

First, knead the clay until it is soft and easy to shape.

2

Then mold the clay into the shape of a pancake.

3

Next, use coils of clay to build the walls of the pot.

4

Finally, smooth the sides of the pot with a scraper.

More About Maria Martinez

Maria Martinez was born in the 1880s.

Maria was one of many generations of Martinez potters.

She won many awards and visited the White House.

Her work appears in museums.

Maria died in 1980.

MAYA
LIN

Maya Lin is an architect and sculptor.

Maya at Yale University

She designs sculptures that are monuments.

Maya in her New York office

When she was in college, Maya Lin entered a contest to design a memorial monument for Vietnam veterans.

Maya shows her final design for the Memorial.

Her design won. It was chosen over hundreds of other designs.

Maya stands on the spot in Washington, D.C., where the Memorial will be built.

The Vietnam Veterans Memorial honors soldiers who fought in the Vietnam War.

Families and friends of the soldiers who died visit the Memorial to see and touch the soldiers' names.

Maya Lin also designed the Civil Rights Memorial in Montgomery, Alabama.

Her monuments honor people.

Maya Lin shows people's thoughts and feelings in the monuments she designs.

In 1993, Maya sits by her sculpture dedicated to women at Yale University.

Let's Explore!

Find the Vietnam Veterans Memorial on the map of Washington, D. C. What is the name of the first street north of the Memorial?

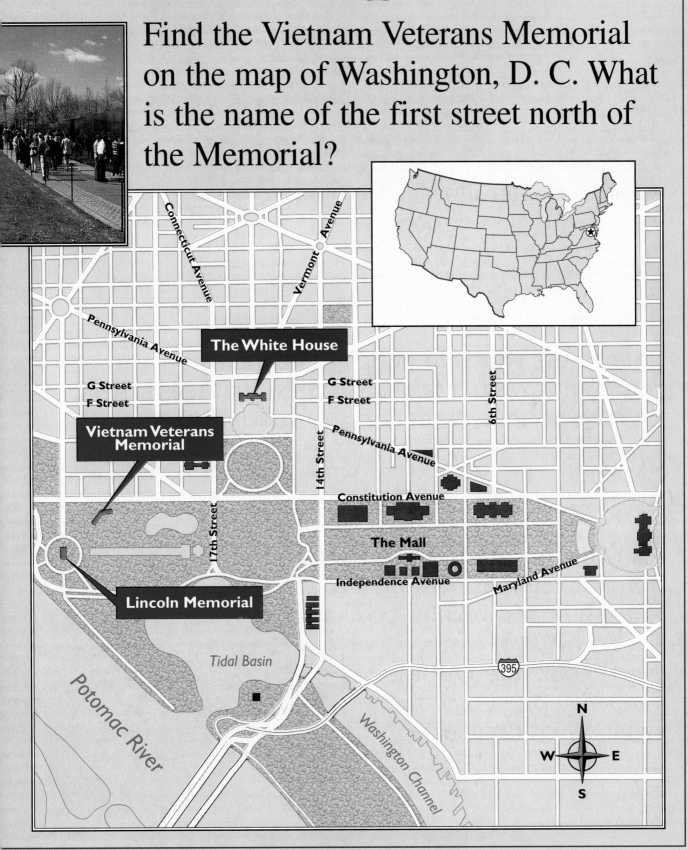

Connecticut Avenue

Vermont Avenue

Pennsylvania Avenue

The White House

G Street

F Street

G Street

F Street

6th Street

Vietnam Veterans Memorial

14th Street

Pennsylvania Avenue

Constitution Avenue

17th Street

The Mall

Lincoln Memorial

Independence Avenue

Maryland Avenue

Tidal Basin

395

Potomac River

Washington Channel

N
W E
S

What Do You Think?

A DESIGN FOR MY FAVORITE PERSON

Draw a picture of a monument for someone special you know. Your monument can show something that person likes or does.

IT IS AN HONOR

You can use words to honor someone who is important to you. Make a word list that tells others why the person you honor is so special.

COIN RUBBINGS

Many people make rubbings from the names on the Vietnam Veterans Memorial to take home with them. You can do a rubbing, too. Place a piece of tissue paper over a coin. Rub the side of the pencil point over the paper. What do you see?

Special Treasures!

Some people leave keepsakes and gifts at the Memorial. Here are some of those objects. These objects and many others are displayed in a museum.

Key Events

Maya Lin was born on October 5, 1959.

Her parents came from China.

She studied at Yale University.

She won the memorial design contest on May 6, 1981.

Maya Lin graduated from college in 1981.

She lives and works in New York City.

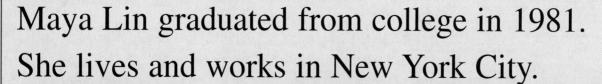

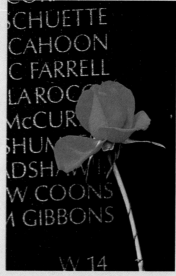

Maya with then Vice President-elect Gore at a ceremony marking the 10th anniversary of the Memorial

Stephen F. Austin

Stephen F. Austin was one of the first leaders in Texas.

Stephen F. Austin is shown in this part of a mural about Texas.

He wanted people to come to live in Texas.

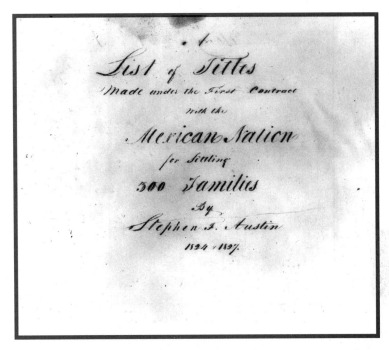

This book listed the names of early settlers of Texas.

The home of a Texan in the 1840s

Hundreds of families settled in Texas with his help.

Stephen F. Austin, shown above and below, helped many settlers get land in Texas.

Austin started schools where children could learn.

A view of Austin, Texas, 1840

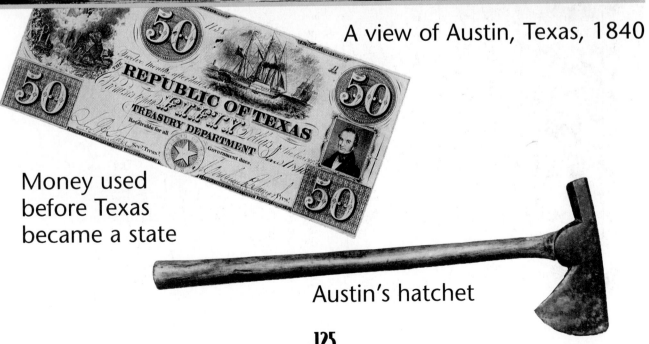

Money used before Texas became a state

Austin's hatchet

At that time, Texas was part of Mexico.

This painting of Austin now hangs in the House of Representatives in Austin, Texas.

Austin helped make Texas independent.

After many battles, the people of Texas won freedom from Mexico.

The Alamo was where a famous battle took place in 1836.

Texans are proud of what Stephen F. Austin did. They call him the "Father of Texas."

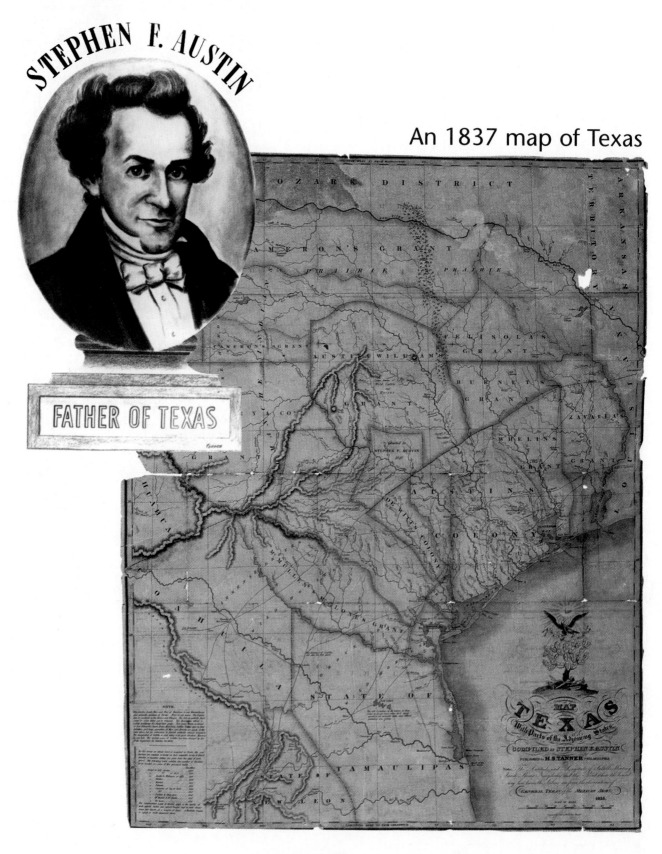

STEPHEN F. AUSTIN

FATHER OF TEXAS

An 1837 map of Texas

Let's Explore!

Look at the map key and map of Texas. What is the name of the capital? What is the Rio Grande?

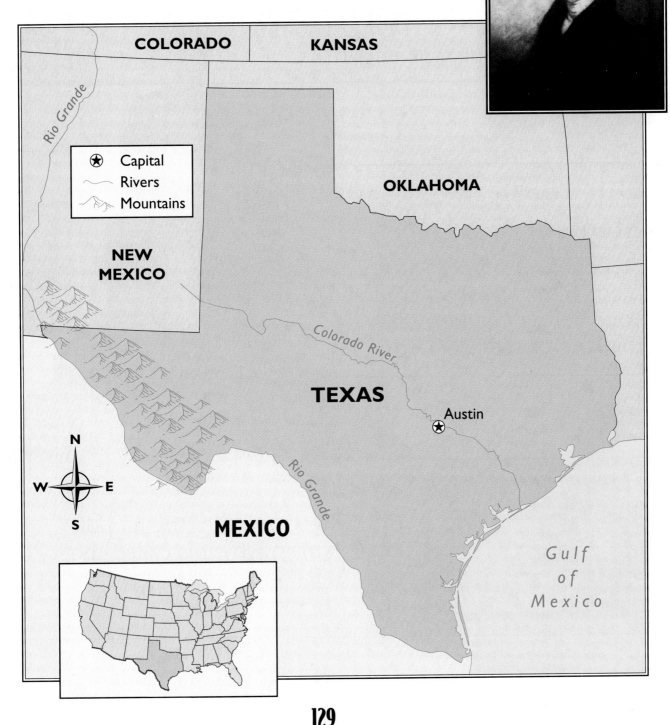

COLORADO

KANSAS

Rio Grande

★ Capital
~ Rivers
⛰ Mountains

OKLAHOMA

NEW MEXICO

Colorado River

TEXAS

Austin

N
W ✦ E
S

Rio Grande

MEXICO

Gulf of Mexico

What Do You Think?

San Jacinto Day

On April 21, 1836, Texans celebrated a great victory over Mexico. It was the beginning of Texas independence. If you were asked to give a speech on that day, what might you say? List some things you would talk about.

Our Hero, Stephen F. Austin

Stephen F. Austin is a Texas hero. Think about a hero for your state. Write why you think he or she is a hero.

State Flag

Write a description of the flag of Texas. Explain why it is called the "Lone Star" flag.

More About Texas!

The state motto is "Friendship." That's because the state's name, *Texas* or *Tejas*, was the Spanish pronunciation of the Caddo word for *friends*.

State gem
topaz

State bird
mockingbird

State large mammal
longhorn

State tree
pecan

TEXAS, OUR TEXAS
Texas, our Texas! All hail
the mighty State!
Texas, our Texas! So
wonderful, so great!
Boldest and grandest,
withstanding every test;
O empire wide and
glorious, you stand
supremely blest.

Verse of the state song

State small mammal
armadillo

State flower
bluebonnet

More About Stephen F. Austin

- Stephen F. Austin was born in 1793.

- Stephen's father, Moses, was given a land grant to settle Texas as a colony. He died before he could settle Texas.

- Stephen settled hundreds of families in the area surrounding what is now Austin.

- Stephen was a lead miner, an editor, and a land agent.

- He died in 1836.

Ellen Ochoa

Ellen Ochoa grew up in California. Today she has an exciting job. She is an astronaut.

First day of sixth grade

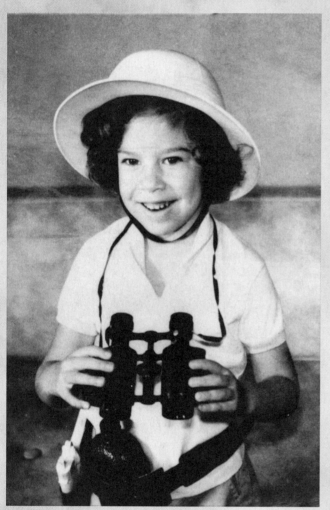

Ellen posing with some birthday gifts

Ellen receiving a Ph.D. degree

She works for the National Aeronautics and Space Administration, or NASA.

Ellen training at the Johnson Space Center for her space flights

Ellen with astronaut Joseph P. Tanner

Ellen Ochoa has gone on two space flights.

On her first space flight, Ellen was part of the crew of *Discovery:* (seated) Steven S. Oswald, Kenneth D. Cameron; (standing) Kenneth D. Cockrell, C. Michael Foale, Ellen Ochoa.

On her second space flight, Ellen wore a patch like this on her space suit.

She studied the sun. She used the shuttle's robot arm to pick up a satellite.

Ochoa aboard *Discovery*

One of Ellen's hobbies is flying a small airplane.

Another hobby is playing the flute. She is shown here at a 1989 recital and taking a break in space.

Ellen likes to speak to children. She tells them to work hard. If they do, they can be what they want to be.

Ellen Ochoa is a good example to others. She worked hard to reach her goals.

Ellen Ochoa likes being an astronaut. "There's nothing else I'd rather be doing," she says.

Let's Explore!

Ellen Ochoa and other astronauts work and study at the Johnson Space Center in Texas. Find the Johnson Space Center on the map. Follow Ellen's route from the Space Center to where the liftoff happened.

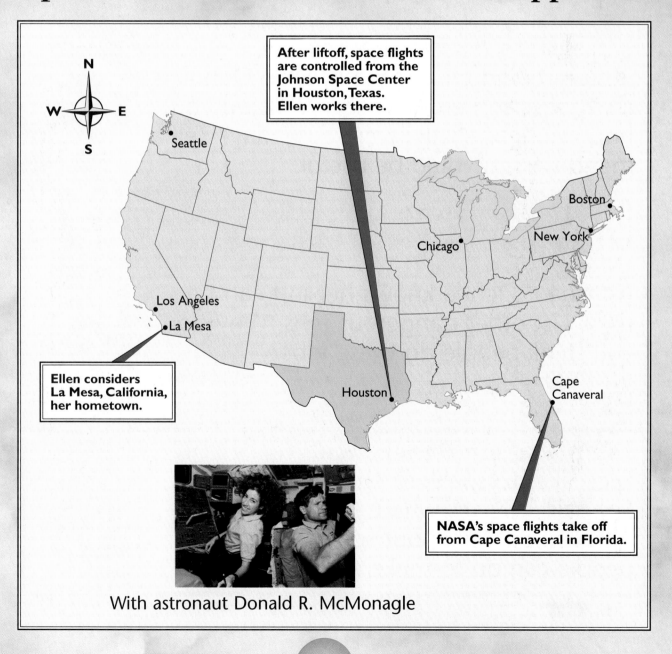

After liftoff, space flights are controlled from the Johnson Space Center in Houston, Texas. Ellen works there.

Ellen considers La Mesa, California, her hometown.

NASA's space flights take off from Cape Canaveral in Florida.

Seattle
Los Angeles
La Mesa
Chicago
Boston
New York
Houston
Cape Canaveral

With astronaut Donald R. McMonagle

What Do You Think?

In Space
Imagine that you have been invited to go along on a space flight. Would you like to go to the moon? To a star? Somewhere else? Write a picture story about it.

Attention, All Inventors!
Besides being an astronaut, Ellen Ochoa is a scientist and an inventor. What do you hope someone will invent someday? Tell a friend why it would be useful.

Danger Ahead!
Astronaut Ochoa knows her job can be risky. List other dangerous jobs. Why do you think people do these jobs?

I Can Make a Difference!
Ellen likes to speak to children in schools. She said, "That's where I can make a difference." Tell about something else people can do to make a difference.

Take a Look!

From the space shuttle, Ellen Ochoa could see exciting views of Earth.

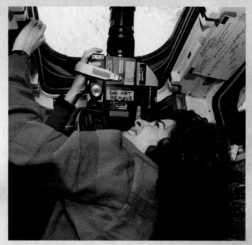

Recording an ocean scene aboard *Discovery*

Mexico and the southeastern United States

Africa, Asia, Europe

Hawaiian Islands

Storm clouds

Key Events

1958 Ellen Ochoa was born in Los Angeles, California.

1975 She graduated from high school in La Mesa, California.

1980 She was top student of San Diego State University in California.

1985 She graduated from Stanford University in Palo Alto, California.

1991 She became an astronaut for NASA.

1993 From April 8 to 17, she was on her first space flight.

1994 From November 3 to 14, she was on her second space flight.

Ellen and her family

The *Discovery* crew

Squanto

©Gary Andrashko/Plimoth Plantation, Inc., 39(t), 47(tl)(tc)(tr)(c)(cr)(bl)(br); The Bettmann Archive, 40; ©Anthony Blake/Tony Stone Images, 44(b); Ralph J. Brunke/ASG Sherman Graphics, Inc., 46; ©Ted Curtin/Plimoth Plantation, Inc., 43; The Granger Collection, New York, 41, 42; Photo courtesy of John Hancock Financial Services, 44(t); ©Breck P. Kent/Animals Animals, 39(b); ©Photo Researchers, Inc., 39(c); Plimoth Plantation, Inc., 47(cl).

Thomas Edison

AP/World Wide Photos, 56; Bettmann, 60(br); The Bettmann Archive, 50(t), 54, 54-55, 55(tl), 59(cl)(cr)(b), 60(tr); The Granger Collection, New York, 51(l)(r), 52, 53, 55(tr); ©Hinous/Gamma Liaison, 50(bl); Image Club Graphics, 49(bkg), 51(br), 58; National Portrait Gallery, Smithsonian Institution/Art Resource, NY, 49; UPI/Bettmann Newsphotos, 59(t).

Martin Luther King, Jr.

AP/World Wide Photos, 72(bl); Bettmann, 66(tl), 67(tr); The Bettmann Archive, 72(br); ©Bob Fitch/Black Star, 70; The Granger Collection, New York, 64(tl); from HM/P. Herbert Private Collection, 64(bl); ©1996 James H. Karales/Peter Arnold, Inc., 69(b); ©Vernon Merritt/Black Star, 67(b); Collection of Picture Research Consultants, 66-67; ©Scheler/Black Star, 71(cr); The Photographs and Prints Division, Schomburg Center, New York Public Library, 71(tr); ©Flip Schulke/ Black Star, 61, 66(b), 71(b); © Schwartz/Liaison International, 62(cl); UPI/Bettmann, 62(tr), 68, 69(cr), 71(cl); UPI/ Bettmann Newsphotos, 61(bkg), 63, 64-65.

George Washington

AP/Wide World Photos, 79(t); Bettmann, 75(tr); The Bettmann Archive, 75(b), 76-77, 83(tr)(br), 84 top to bottom(3); The Granger Collection, New York, 74(t), 75(tl), 77(t), 78(t)(bl), 80, 83(tl)(bl), 84 top to bottom(1)(2)(4)(5); ©Wesley Hitt/Liaison International, 82; © James H. Pickerell/Liaison International, 81; PhotoDisc Images ©1995 PhotoDisc, Inc., 79(b); ©1982 Ted Spiegel/Black Star, 77(b); ©Stock Montage, 74(b), 78(br); ©SuperStock, 73.

Gary Soto

Ralph J. Brunke/ASG Sherman Graphics, Inc., 94(tr); ©Marvin Collins, 85(bl); Courtesy of Gary Soto, 85(r), 86, 87, 88, 89, 90, 91, 92, 95, 96; ©SuperStock, 94(tl).

Maria Martinez

©1996 Cradoc Bagshaw, 97, 99(tr), 102(r), 104(b), 108; Photo by T.L. Bierwer, Courtesy Department Library Services/American Museum of Natural History, Neg. #297352, 102(tl); Photo by Clyde Fisher, Courtesy Department Library Services/American Museum of Natural History, Neg. #297353, 102(cl), Neg. #297355, 100(t), Neg. #297358, 104(cl), Neg. #297360, 104(tr); Photo by H.S. Rice, Courtesy Department Library Services/American Museum of Natural History, Neg. #280323, 98(t); Photo by Rota, Courtesy Department Library Services/American Museum of Natural History, Neg. #332066, 105(t); ©Stephen Trimble, 98(l), 98-99, 100-101, 101, 103, 106.

Maya Lin

Photography by: E. "Manny" Abraben, 110(br), 111, 112(br), 113(r)(b); AP/Wide World Photo, 110-111, 113(c), 120(br); Ralph J. Brunke/ASG Sherman Graphics, Inc., 118(t); ©1987 Jim Bryant/Gamma Liaison, 119(tl); ©Thomas S. England/Photo Researchers, Inc., 115(t); ©1992 Claus Guglberger/Black Star, 120(c); ©1983 Richard Howard/Black Star, 120(tr); ©1992 Richard Howard/Black Star, 109; ©Keith Lanpher/Liaison International, 116(t), 120(bl); Michael Marsland/Yale University-Office of Public Affairs, 110(tl), 116(b), 120(cr); ©1992 Forest McMullin/Black Star, 109(bkg); ©1992 Christopher Morris/Black Star, 118(b); ©1993 Naoki Okamoto/Black Star, 120(cl); ©Margo Taussig Pinkerton/Liaison International, 117; UPI/Bettmann, 114(b), 114-115, 115(br); UPI/Corbis-Bettmann, 112(t); UPI/Bettmann Newsphotos, 114(tl); Photography by Vasquez, Claudio and Z., Taran/Turner Publishing, Inc., 119(tc)(tr)(cl)(c)(bl)(bc)(br), Yale University-Office of Public Affairs, 110(bl).